Killing Public Higher Education

Killing Public Higher Education
The Arms Race for Research Prestige

David L. Stocum

AMSTERDAM • BOSTON • HEIDELBERG • LONDON
NEW YORK • OXFORD • PARIS • SAN DIEGO
SAN FRANCISCO • SINGAPORE • SYDNEY • TOKYO
Academic press is an imprint of Elsevier

Academic Press is an imprint of Elsevier
The Boulevard, Langford Lane, Kidlington, Oxford, OX5 1GB, UK
225 Wyman Street, Waltham, MA 02451, USA

First published 2013

Copyright © 2013 Elsevier Inc. All rights reserved.

No part of this publication may be reproduced or transmitted in any form or by any means, electronic or mechanical, including photocopying, recording, or any information storage and retrieval system, without permission in writing from the publisher. Details on how to seek permission, further information about the Publisher's permissions policies and our arrangement with organizations such as the Copyright Clearance Center and the Copyright Licensing Agency, can be found at our website: www.elsevier.com/permissions

This book and the individual contributions contained in it are protected under copyright by the Publisher (other than as may be noted herein).

Notices
Knowledge and best practice in this field are constantly changing. As new research and experience broaden our understanding, changes in research methods, professional practices, or medical treatment may become necessary.

Practitioners and researchers must always rely on their own experience and knowledge in evaluating and using any information, methods, compounds, or experiments described herein. In using such information or methods they should be mindful of their own safety and the safety of others, including parties for whom they have a professional responsibility.

To the fullest extent of the law, neither the Publisher nor the authors, contributors, or editors, assume any liability for any injury and/or damage to persons or property as a matter of products liability, negligence or otherwise, or from any use or operation of any methods, products, instructions, or ideas contained in the material herein.

British Library Cataloguing in Publication Data
A catalogue record for this book is available from the British Library

Library of Congress Cataloging-in-Publication Data
A catalog record for this book is available from the Library of Congress

ISBN: 978-0-12-411510-1

For information on all Academic Press publications
visit our website at store.elsevier.com

This book has been manufactured using Print On Demand technology. Each copy is produced to order and is limited to black ink. The online version of this book will show color figures where appropriate.

Working together to grow
libraries in developing countries

www.elsevier.com | www.bookaid.org | www.sabre.org

ELSEVIER   BOOK AID International   Sabre Foundation

Transferred to Digital Printing in 2013

CONTENTS

Acknowledgments vii
About the Author ix

**Killing Public Higher Education: The Arms Race
for Research Prestige** 1
Introduction 1
The Addiction to Research Prestige Contributes
to the Increasing Costs of Higher Education 2
Portrait of the Flagships 5
   Origin and Emergence 5
   The Flagship Culture Today 7
Rationales for Mission Differentiation 12
   Quality Is Synonymous with an Exclusive
   Research Mission 12
   Stratification of Students Reflects Their Intellectual
   Status and Capability 12
Rankism: The Underlying Disease of the
Caste System 14
   Schemes to Privatize Public Flagships 15
   The AAU Snob Factor 16
   Graduate Programs 17
   Community Colleges 17
Research Prestige and Athletic Prestige: Brothers
Under the Skin 18
The Future of Higher Education 22
   Business as Usual 23
   Tweak Around the Edges 25
   Spin off Research and Graduate Education 26
   Restructure the System 27
Defining the Purpose of Undergraduate Education 30
The Urban University as a Model for the
Twenty-First Century 32
References 33

ACKNOWLEDGMENTS

I thank the following individuals who read and commented on this essay: John Barlow, Gerald Bepko, Jo Ann Cameron, Robert Hammerle, Ellen Heber-Katz, Steve Hinterberger, P.E. MacAllister, Gerald Michael, Paul Raikes, Michael Schleuter, Laura Stocum, Jack Waaler, Romayne Wicklund, and Gunther Zupanc.

ABOUT THE AUTHOR

David L. Stocum is Professor of Biology and Co-Director, Indiana University Center for Regenerative Biology and Medicine, and Dean Emeritus, School of Science, Indiana University-Purdue University Indianapolis (IUPUI). Prior to his work at IUPUI, he was Professor of Cell and Structural Biology at the University of Illinois at Urbana-Champaign.

Killing Public Higher Education: The Arms Race for Research Prestige

INTRODUCTION

In 1968, armed with a PhD from a distinguished private research university, the University of Pennsylvania, I began a faculty career in a public flagship research university, the University of Illinois at Urbana-Champaign (UIUC). Two decades later, I became dean of science at a large urban public university, Indiana University-Purdue University at Indianapolis (IUPUI), a position I held for 15 years. The contrast between these two types of public universities brought into sharp focus for me the fact that American public higher education is a caste system disguised under the euphemism of "mission differentiation." The system is dominated in each state by one or two massive flagship universities characterized by a culture of snobbish exclusivity and entitlement that compete in a frantic arms race for money and research prestige rankings. The flagships treat their subordinate campuses and other state-supported universities with patronizing condescension, if not outright contempt.

In this essay, I argue that whereas research itself is an important function of universities, the competition among the public flagships for more money, research prestige, and power, and the imposition of mission differentiation on their subordinate and other public universities, is dysfunctional and does not well serve the needs of our society in the twenty-first century. The addiction to research prestige is a chronic impairment that contributes to the ever-increasing costs of higher education and the devaluing of undergraduate education. This problem has been extensively documented, particularly over the past 20 years, it can no longer be denied even by the most ardent apologists and cannot be solved by schemes to preserve the status quo or by tweaking around the edges. The most viable solution is a fundamental restructuring of public higher education in which the flagships play a less dominating role and imposed mission differentiation is ended. This will require the flagships (as well as other state universities who wish to emulate them) to make undergraduate education a much higher priority, make research significance *per se*, not research prestige rankings the objective, and be willing to collaborate in state and regional educational and research networks to produce the kinds of graduates and new knowledge that states, and the nation and society in general, need to flourish.

This text evolved from two previous publications by the author (Stocum, 2000, 2001). While writing it, I read the book titled *Higher Education? How Colleges Are Wasting Our Money and Failing Our Kids—and What We Can Do About it* by Andrew Hacker and Claudia Dreifus (2010). This volume is the broadest treatment of the good, the bad, and the ugly in higher education today, and I recommend it to anyone interested in the subject.

THE ADDICTION TO RESEARCH PRESTIGE CONTRIBUTES TO THE INCREASING COSTS OF HIGHER EDUCATION

Tuition fees at all state-supported universities has increased at rates far greater than the rise in household income or the consumer price index over the past two decades. Many graduates are entering a weak job market carrying heavy debt and a feeling of having been shortchanged academically. The drivers of the tuition increases have been enumerated many times: declining state support, increasing salaries and benefits of administrators and faculty (although increases for the latter pale in comparison to those of the former), yearly increases in the cost of health insurance, subsidies for athletic programs, and legal fees (Hacker and Dreifus, 2010; Kamenetz, 2010a; Schrecker, 2010). Then there is the increasing specialization and proliferation of administrative positions with their attendant staff that did not exist three, or even two, decades ago, to promote the interests of various student groups, enforce an ever-increasing number of regulatory compliances (Lesher and Fluharty, 2012), and generate numbers for every conceivable category of university operations that might convince state legislators of university accountability, and influence national rankings (Tuchman, 2009). These cost drivers need to be addressed and reduced.

All types of public universities have shown similar percentage increases in tuition fees over the past decade. However, the absolute amount of tuition charged by public flagships is substantially more than universities lower in the caste system, and this differential is related to their extensive research and graduate education programs. In addition, many public flagships actively recruit significant numbers of out-of-state and international students who they charge two to three times more tuition than in-state students, thus creating a large gap in tuition revenue between themselves and other state institutions that cater mainly to in-state students.

The addiction to research prestige is a driver of tuition increases in flagship universities because it is costly and tightly coupled to the tenure and promotion system (see Hacker and Dreifus, 2010, and many others). To obtain tenure and advance in rank, professors must obtain research grants that result in an acceptable output of peer-reviewed articles. The direct costs of a typical grant provide salaries and benefits to professors, graduate students, and postdoctoral fellows, as well as for the purchase of equipment and supplies. There is, however, good grant money and bad grant money. Good grant money is that which adds indirect cost recovery (ICR) income of over 50% of personnel costs to each grant to defray the overhead costs of administration, space, energy, and water required to conduct the research. Bad grant money pays only the direct costs of research. Deans control most of the ICR funds and use them for any number of research-related purposes, such as laboratory start-up funding for newly-hired professors or to help pay for new or renovated space. In the science, technology, engineering and mathematics (STEM) disciplines, start-up costs can range from minimal (mathematics) to hundreds of thousands and even millions of dollars for research in biology, chemistry, physics, and computer science. Millions more are put into the construction of new facilities, banking on a steady stream of ICR income from faculty-generated grants over an extended period of time. In the past, many new facilities at private research universities have been built by negotiating ICR rates of over 100%.

Although grants are one of the three to four main revenue streams of research universities, they never cover the total costs of research. Tuition and fee income and state appropriations, which are intended primarily to support undergraduate education, are also used to support research. Part of the tuition and state appropriation income at research universities is used to employ highly-paid vice presidents and vice chancellors for research and their assistants to develop and implement research strategies and policies, as well as to support deans of graduate schools and their staff to do the same for graduate programs. In addition, grants and contracts units are essential to process grant proposals and awards and keep track of grant accounts. Collectively, these functions are a significant cost driver.

Another cost driver is the fact that research faculty teach less in order to free up the time required to continually write multiple grant proposals and supervise the research of postdoctoral fellows and graduate students. Rather than hire full-time faculty to fill in the instructional gaps, research universities hire nontenure-track part-time faculty to save money. According to a report by the American Association of Colleges and Universities (AACU), 68% of the faculty positions at all degree-granting institutions are nontenure-track appointments; the figure is 48% at public doctoral-granting/research universities (Bergom and Waltman, 2009). Many of these faculty members are excellent teachers, but they carry heavy work responsibilities, are paid much less on average than tenure-track faculty, have few or no health benefits, and get little respect within their universities. Among tenure-track faculty members, those who have successful research programs are paid much more and command more respect than those who focus on teaching or service. These differentials in prestige have led to significant disparities in salary and benefits for the same academic ranks within institutions, leading to the creation of two-tier faculties. Across institutions, these disparities follow exactly the mission differentiation hierarchy of flagship: secondary research university: comprehensive university: community college.

The situation is becoming even more exacerbated as the competition for research grants gets ever more intense in the face of static, or even potentially decreasing, federal research budgets. Although rigorous selection keeps turnover of tenure-track faculty relatively low at flagships, assistant professors who cannot get grants or fail to publish the requisite number of papers within 5 years are denied tenure and their positions are terminated. They are replaced by new research assistant professors, most likely at higher salaries and requiring another round of start-up funding. Furthermore, research stars are individual entrepreneurs who often have little loyalty to their institution and are continually for sale to other institutions who can offer them better salaries and research space. Lastly, tenured professors who fail to get grants renewed over a period of time become a financial liability if their teaching duties are not increased.

What is wrong with this picture is not, as some would have it, the engagement of universities in research *per se*. Research that addresses interesting and significant questions, although perhaps without immediate practical application, is well worth supporting in any university that can afford to engage in it. The real problem is the perpetual and costly arms race for *research prestige* that has become an end in itself, where rank, size, money, and power are used for self-aggrandizement and to deny aspirations and respect to "inferior" universities. This focus on research rankings and the financial and social costs they exact has been extensively documented (Alpert, 1993; Anderson, 1992; Boyte and Hollander, 1999; Hacker and Dreifus, 2010; Kamenetz, 2010a; Parker et al., 2001; Rhode, 2006; Schrecker, 2010; Smith, 1990; Sperber, 2000; Tuchman, 2009, and many others). In the guise of mission differentiation, it has over time resulted in enormous resource inequality between the flagships and other types of state universities, and generated ever-rising costs.

PORTRAIT OF THE FLAGSHIPS
Origin and Emergence
The Morrill Act of 1862 established many of the first public state universities that were, along with public institutions founded earlier, destined to become today's flagships. Their purpose was to educate the sons and daughters of the state's working class citizens and to produce research and technology of benefit to the industrial and agricultural needs of the states. This broad focus on research, educational, agricultural, and industrial needs defined the land grant universities until the end of the Second World War. Their low tuition, subsidized by the state, greatly increased access to higher education. There is no question that in this form these universities have made tremendous contributions to the agricultural, scientific, technological, and civic and cultural strength of the nation, to the upward mobility of its citizens, and to the building of a more equitable and opportunity-filled society.

The original public universities were the largest in their states. During the Second World War, they performed research related to weapons development. In July 1945, Vannevar Bush published a treatise titled "Science, the Endless Frontier," in which he promulgated a long-term vision of government-supported scientific research to increase the economic strength, security, and international prestige of the nation. Driven by the Cold War with the Soviet Union, this vision transformed the structure and function of public higher education. The land grant universities and other state universities underwent a dramatic expansion in enrollment due to the influx of returning servicemen on the G.I. bill. Weary of the experiences of war, this highly motivated generation of students was the epitome of what both private and public universities could do to promote success and prosperity. Every generation since has wanted its children to be university educated, resulting in a continually expanding demand for higher education.

A massive influx of federal money into the land grant universities expanded research in all disciplines, particularly in the STEM fields, but also in the arts and humanities. Graduate education became a top priority, partly to meet the labor demands of faculty research programs, partly to meet the rising demand for faculty to teach the swelling ranks of undergraduate and graduate students, and partly to fill the needs generated by corporate expansion. American graduate schools became the envy of the world. Large numbers of foreign graduate students have studied in them to become the academic, industrial, and government leaders of their own countries.

Perhaps inevitably, the state and federal research funds poured into the land grant universities after the war also led to the creation of the academic caste system. The land grant universities were defined as flagships, entitled to more state dollars than other public universities and aspiring to the same academic prestige accorded to the elite private research universities. To get it, they competed fiercely for superstar research faculty and graduate students. However, as the research function took precedence in the flagships and elsewhere, the overall quality of undergraduate education declined (Alpert, 1993; Arum and Roska, 2011; Katz, 2002; Nichol, 2008).

Until the early 1960s, when enrollments began to overwhelm capacity, most land grant state universities would accept anyone who graduated in the upper two-thirds of their high school class. Once accepted, the student was responsible for doing well enough to graduate. But as the economic need for education beyond high school increased and the number of college-going students soared, the research and teaching missions of the flagships came into conflict. The solution was to become more selective in admissions. The rationale was that the brightest and best prepared undergraduate students would not need as much attention from professors, who were then free to spend most of their time on research and graduate education. The increased research prestige of the university could then be used to attract faculty who would help build up the capacity to generate more federal research dollars. The less-selective students who once formed part of the flagship clientele could go to lesser public institutions that were focused more on teaching.

This process resulted in stratification of the state universities, which then became institutionalized as "mission differentiation." Mission differentiation meant not only the stratification of students, but also a stratification of academic pay, with flagship administrators and faculty on the high end. Most of all, it meant that respect was stratified. Publications and grant awards became the primary basis for professorial advancement and reward in the flagships and by default became the standards by which all of a state's public universities are measured and ranked, whether they like it or not.

The Flagship Culture Today

Today's flagships keep a jealous eye on one another and compete fiercely for research rankings based on numbers of PhDs produced, papers published, and federal research dollars awarded. Some flagships are less prestigious than others. Because they strive to join the ranks of the more prestigious, they are called "wannabes." Gaye Tuchman (2009) has described in detail the inner workings of one of these institutions in her book *Wannabe U*. Comprehensive universities aiming to elevate their research prestige in order to gain some measure of respect are called wannabes engaging in "mission creep" by the flagships, state legislatures, and higher education authorities. Even the most prestigious public flagships, however, are themselves wannabes, striving for the same research status as the private research universities.

The public flagship universities have little sense of community outside their athletic conference or even their own walls. The flagships claim to be serious about excellence in teaching and undergraduate education, but in reality have little interest in this core university mission. They graduate a high percentage of their students, but their teaching function has been increasingly relegated to lecturers, teaching assistants, adjuncts, and tenured professors considered to be research failures. Undergraduate teaching has been devalued to the point where the prestige of faculty members is inversely proportional to the amount of undergraduate teaching they do (Hacker and Dreifus, 2010; Katz, 2002; Wilson, 2010). I distinctly recall being counseled by a savvy colleague during my first year on the faculty at the University of Illinois to "spend as little time with the undergraduates as possible." Under these conditions, it is little wonder that the quality of undergraduate education at public flagships is marginal at best and that professors have become increasingly isolated from each other and their students, and ignore concern for the common good.

Questions have been raised for decades as to whether the money spent by flagships on research prestige brings returns other than a public image used to recruit students and faculty. Many authors have argued that only a small fraction of university research has had any lasting impact. Smith (1990) ventured the opinion that the vast majority of research conducted in universities is worthless. Quoting Anderson (1992), "Taken as a whole, academic research and writing is the greatest intellectual fraud of the twentieth century." According to Donald Kennedy, former President of Stanford University, "The overproduction of routine scholarship is one of the most egregious aspects of contemporary academic life: It tends to conceal really important work by its sheer volume; it wastes time and valuable resources" (quoted in Anderson, 1992).

There is considerable truth in these statements. Millions of papers are published each year, and it is true that only a small percentage is significant enough to make a major or even minor advance in understanding and/or application. Depending on one's definition of significance, it could be argued that only Nobel Prize winners have conducted significant research. This of course is not true; there is a second (and even third) level of innovative scholarship, involving a much larger number of researchers that complement the top level, and which fills in knowledge gaps and expands the knowledge base essential for advancement. Regardless, the publications representing the actual advancement of knowledge are still only a small fraction of the total academic output.

On the positive side, this research has deepened our understanding of, and ability to manipulate, the natural world. We have learned much about the origins of the universe and of ourselves, gained an understanding of the molecular processes underlying health and disease, gone to the moon, and sent rovers to Mars and probes into deep space. We have developed highly sophisticated surgical techniques, vaccines, and antibiotics. We have advanced our understanding of cellular and developmental biology, and have discovered how to make ordinary skin cells become stem cells for regenerative purposes. The existence of so much pedestrian research that does not really extend previous knowledge can be tied directly to the flagship-driven "publish or perish" and "grant or gone" syndrome, which is in turn fueled by the competition for research rankings.

Implicit in the concept of mission differentiation is the idea that only flagship faculty should or can publish premier research papers. They would have us believe that it is not they who drown the academic world in routine scholarship, but their inferiors in nonflagship institutions. In reality, public flagship universities publish a great deal of pedestrian research alongside outstanding research. Many groundbreaking discoveries have been made in these universities, but many others have been made in comprehensive and regional universities as well. The problem with the flagships is not that they do not make original discoveries, but deny that anyone else does or should, about which I will say more ahead.

A major problem created by the flagships is the overproduction of PhDs, who are expected to publish their dissertation research even if they have no intention of making a career of research. Bruce Alberts, former President of the National Academy of Sciences, points out that the number of PhDs produced, even in the biomedical sciences, far outstrips demand (Alberts, 2010)—there are too many scientists relative to resources (Cyranoski et al., 2011; Martinson, 2007). In fact, the carrying capacity of the federal-granting system was reached long ago, in the 1970s (Alpert, 1993). The overproduction of PhDs is in part responsible for an increasing number of research faculty positions at all types of universities. On the plus side, this could strengthen the research function of the nonflagship state universities, potentially increasing their opportunities for discovery and innovation (see ahead). At the same time, however, there will be a proportional increase in competition for grant funds, and many PhDs will exit the fields for which they were trained.

In a 1989 publication titled *"Values Added: Undergraduate Education at the Universities of the CIC,"* the Committee on Institutional Cooperation (consisting of all the Big Ten universities plus the University of Chicago) argued that one of the values added by the research university is a linkage between research and teaching excellence. Although the wording was careful, the implication was that excellence in research has a positive correlation with excellence in teaching. At least one meta-study has indicated that there is zero correlation between excellence in research and teaching (not a *negative* correlation as is sometimes reported) (Hattie and Marsh, 1996). Quoting Hattie and Marsh (2004), this means that "...there can be as many excellent teachers and researchers as there are excellent teachers, excellent researchers, and not-so-excellent teachers or researchers." Good teaching is hard work requiring not only a passion for and deep understanding of subject matter, but also organizational skills, skill, and innovation in engaging students, awareness of and willingness to explore new ways of teaching, and a positive attitude that treats students as an investment in the future. Research has been found to be a positive pedagogical tool, however, in undergraduate research programs designed to show students how to identify interesting questions and find ways to answer them (Undergraduate Research as a Deep Learning Experience, College of Arts and Sciences Undergraduate Research Advisory Committee, Winthrop University, 2006; MacDougall, 2012).

The CIC also claimed in their publication that in addition to the evaluation of research in tenure and promotion decisions "...we also require clear evidence of teaching ability; and both are valued and rewarded." During my career at Illinois, I never saw any evidence that good teaching was valued or rewarded, at least in my discipline of the biological sciences; the only thing that counted for tenure and promotion was externally funded research and publications. My colleagues at other flagship institutions have made similar observations.

In an intriguing working paper titled "Why do Institutions of Higher Education Reward Research While Selling Education?," Remler and Pema (2009) explore several hypotheses relevant to this question. One is that research acts as a mechanism to favor high ability over low ability students. If faculty researchers make education more costly to lower ability students by being bad teachers, lower ability students will be eliminated more efficiently from the university and fewer resources will be wasted on undergraduate education. This mechanism, however, could have negative financial implications related to tuition income. Closer to the mark in my view is their hypothesis that research raises the consumption value of institutional educational offerings to students. In other words, research is supported because it confers individual and institutional prestige valued by students and their parents. Consumption value and prestige assume that students and their parents are as rank-conscious as the institutions themselves, an assumption backed by a great deal of data (Hacker and Dreifus, 2010).

The pursuit of research prestige has engendered a toxic flagship culture that can bring out the worst in people. Too many flagship faculty, administrators, and trustees come off as arrogant, narcissistic snobs, lacking in conscience, and integrity. Anderson (1992) stated flatly, "The death of integrity in the heart of higher education is the root cause of the educational troubles which afflict us today," an indictment echoed by many other observers of higher education, internal and external to the academy. As a faculty member at UIUC, I saw how UIUC faculty and administrators looked down on the University of Illinois at Chicago (UIC), and I experienced the flagship arrogance and snobbery directly as a dean at IUPUI in relation to Indiana University Bloomington (IUB) and Purdue University West Lafayette (PUWL). Some years ago, a colleague shared with me a letter he had received from a highly acclaimed colleague who summed up the culture of the public flagship he had just left as follows: "...minimal good will, in-turned protectiveness of self, intense competitiveness, glee in the belittlement of others, insecure self-esteem, the plodding progress through life with little of its joy, the loss of ideals of integrity, of concern for others, of the beauty of life and sharing it with others." Despite having many wonderful colleagues in a number of public flagships, I think this is a fair description of the nature of the beast.

To summarize to this point, the message from the elitists and governing bodies in higher education is clear: the worth and value of a public university depends on the image, prestige, money, and power conferred by its degree of research status. The euphemism for this caste system is "mission differentiation"—the assignment of different academic missions to universities based on the presumed intellectual quality of their students and faculty, and the apportioning of resources according to that presumption.

RATIONALES FOR MISSION DIFFERENTIATION

Mission differentiation is a historical artifact of the Morrill Act that has become institutionalized. The flagships were established first, were the largest, and already had research-oriented faculty when the federal money tap was turned on. As research became the measuring stick for prestige, the smaller state universities were at a disadvantage and were relegated to lower status that has been maintained ever since. However, mission differentiation has been directly *imposed* on the subordinate campuses of systems by their flagships, higher education commissions, and legislatures. In recent years, some of these campuses, particularly urban ones, have grown rapidly and recruited outstanding research faculty, and are now viewed as a threat to the research hegemony of the flagships.

There are two general rationales used by legislators, higher education commissions, and flagships to justify mission differentiation.

Quality Is Synonymous with an Exclusive Research Mission

Although the flagships would claim that "quality" means both teaching and research, the internal truth is that it refers only to research. They see the flagship mission as research, and the nonflagship mission as teaching. The flagships have argued that fostering a research mission in nonflagship institutions wastes tax dollars that could better go to them. This means, however, that a great deal of diversified research talent and innovation that would otherwise exist outside the flagships is lost. Even more importantly, it means that the flagships view teaching as a secondary activity. Because these views are aided and abetted by the funding formulas of state legislatures, the task of increasing the numbers of college graduates, particularly in STEM areas, falls on the less-well-funded institutions and is thus compromised.

Stratification of Students Reflects Their Intellectual Status and Capability

Mission differentiation assumes that populations of students at each level of the caste system are homogenous, with flagship universities enrolling only the best and brightest students. Thus it makes sense to have different tiers of public universities based on these arbitrary notions of ability and aspiration. This is a flawed argument for several reasons.

First, student populations today do not actually conform to these stratifications, if they ever did. The evidence suggests that the supposed inferiority of students in the comprehensive and urban universities is a myth and that student populations at all levels of the caste system are similar in their heterogeneity of talent and preparation for university-level work, although differences in persistence have been noted (Culpepper, 2006). The data indicate that flagships bias their student population toward more economically-advantaged students (Carey, 2012; Hacker and Dreifus, 2010; Haycock et al., 2010; Nichol, 2008). Such bias is leading to ever-increasing social and economic polarization throughout the higher education system (Carnavale and Strohl, 2011; Kahlenberg, 2012; Quiggen, 2011).

Second, the flagship research universities are much bigger and wealthier than other public institutions. By my estimate, however, they enroll perhaps 20% of the total number of undergraduate students admitted to public universities. It makes little economic sense to treat the other 80%, which by sheer numbers will form the bulk of the work force, including CEO positions, as "inferior," while providing the relatively advantaged students of the flagships with every available prestige marker.

Third, it makes even less social sense to say that this 80% should not have, or does not need, a high-quality educational experience, or that the faculties who teach these students should not aspire to excellence. Access to mediocrity is of little value. But that is the message of mission differentiation: these students and the faculty who teach them do not deserve this kind of quality. This view was vividly illustrated for me when as a dean I invited the Commissioner of the Indiana Commission for Higher Education to a meeting of my community advisory council. At this meeting, I made a presentation on the integrated academic and research advances our School of Science had made. The Commissioner, who was openly against IUPUI being anything more than a remedial campus, did not believe we had (or needed) quality academic programs and wanted to know how we had made these advances. Part of my answer was that we hired faculty better than ourselves. "Well," came the stunning response, "*you* shouldn't be hiring all those good faculty."

Fourth, Astin (1999) has observed that contrary to working for the benefit of students, segregating them into institutions whose missions are differentiated on the basis of flagship and state-prescribed activities, and resources, actually sends the message that we do not value their education. It ensures that the differences between the haves and have-nots in our society will be perpetuated and exacerbated. Reich (2000) has pointed out how increasing selectivity in the way higher education resources are allocated by state legislatures has widened existing inequalities, due to the disparity between the supply and demand for workers with the education and skills needed to meet the demands for innovation in today's economy. More fundamentally, such inequalities foster a culture of low aspirations that negatively affects the economy of a state.

RANKISM: THE UNDERLYING DISEASE OF THE CASTE SYSTEM

The singular feature defining today's public flagships is the pursuit of research prestige for the sake of rankings. There is nothing wrong with aspiring to be elite in the sense of being the best you can be at understanding and solving research problems, and developing the ability of students to argue and write effectively, understand basic mathematics, and become independent lifelong learners. Nor is there anything wrong with high rank earned on the basis of performance. No one would claim that Olympic medalists do not deserve their rank, and the same is true in other endeavors of life where stellar performance has earned respect and admiration. The difference is that, unlike Olympic athletes, universities have various ways of gaming the system to enhance their rank.

The disease underlying the pathological prestige seeking of the flagship universities is rankism. Rankism is a term coined by Robert W. Fuller, former President of Antioch College, in his 2004 book *Somebodies and Nobodies: Overcoming the Abuse of Rank*. Rankism is defined as the use of rank to demean the accomplishments, value, and dignity of others. Fuller makes a powerful case that-isms such as elitism, racism, and sexism, are all manifestations of rankism. Individuals and organizations use rankism to strip the ranks below them of dignity and self-worth in order to feed their own sense of self-importance. The more me, the less you! Fuller's book should be a must-read for anyone in charge of any sort of organization that wishes to be maximally effective without resorting to unethical practices.

Rankism flourishes in our flagship public universities, aided and abetted by educational governing bodies and legislatures. To these institutions, elite does not mean simply being the best you can be, but must involve actively demeaning institutions with lower research prestige. Their arrogance, dismissiveness, and snobbishness are the hallmarks of a corrosive combination of insecurity and ambition that erodes the real purpose and value of higher education. I have known faculty at rankist flagship universities who accomplished very little, yet felt themselves superior to truly accomplished faculty at nonflagships (the halo effect!).

The power of rankism in higher education is reflected in several different ways.

Schemes to Privatize Public Flagships

Several public flagships have aspired to attain the ranks of globally-elite private universities such as Harvard, MIT, Stanford, Oxford, and Cambridge. Most have not attained this distinction and likely never will unless they abandon their land grant origin, mission, and values, dissociate themselves from their state systems and become completely privatized or federally supported (Skinner and Miller, 2012). Many flagship faculty and administrators who support privatization believe that if they were free of their obligations as a state university, and from the taint of their regional campuses, they could better promote their own interests and prestige (Gose, 2002; Rhodes, 2006). As one person commented on Inside Higher Ed, the University of Wisconsin at Madison does not compete with Oshkosh and Whitewater, but with Berkeley.

Northwestern is the only private university in the Big Ten. The University of Wisconsin at Madison is the only public Big Ten flagship that has actually made steps toward privatization. In 2011, a deal was proposed between the governor of Wisconsin and the Chancellor of UWM to separate UWM from the Wisconsin system of regional universities (Berrett, 2011; Carey, 2011; Julius, 2011). The proposal was defeated but will likely be resurrected as opportunity presents. The University of Maryland College Park and the University of North Carolina Chapel Hill have put forward similar unsuccessful proposals to their state legislatures.

Financial considerations are usually given as the reason for privatization. Many flagships would argue that based on the declining percentage of their budget provided by state taxpayers, they are nearly private now, but this argument is somewhat misleading. State support for public universities in absolute dollars is about what it was at its peak in the 1980s and 1990 (Baskin, 2012a). The level of state appropriation as a percent of the total budget and per student has indeed declined since that time, in some states over 40% per student. However, it can be argued that a large part of this decline is due to increases in enrollments, university income from other sources (particularly higher tuition from out-of-state students), and in expenditures. The data indicate that overall, even in today's harsh economic climate, the flagships have significantly more financial and physical resources than other public universities. It is actually rankism that underlies privatization efforts.

The AAU Snob Factor

The Association of American Universities (AAU) plays a major role in the flagship arms race for research prestige. Founded in 1900 by 14 PhD-granting universities, the purpose of the AAU is to promote strong programs in academic research and scholarship and graduate and professional education (see Wikipedia entry). Strengthening undergraduate education is also listed as a purpose, but it is clear that research is the main focus of the organization. Membership is exclusive and by invitation only. Invitation is based on four criteria: research spending, the percentage of faculty who are members of the National Academies, faculty awards, and citations. Research spending is normed to the size of the school so the number that counts is research dollars per faculty member (Nelson, 2011). Annual institutional dues are $80,500. The AAU lobbies in Washington for research funding for its members, which number 34 public universities and 25 private ones.

AAU membership is a powerful opiate in the research prestige arms race. Current members and wannabes will do anything in their power to maintain or acquire membership. The AAU weeds from its ranks members perceived as eroding the prestige of the organization. Thus in 2012, the AAU ejected the University of Nebraska at Lincoln because research dollars generated per faculty member were deemed insufficient to retain membership (Baskin, 2011; Nelson, 2011). The problem was that the nationally ranked University of Nebraska Medical Center is in Omaha, and its research dollars are reported separately from the Lincoln campus. Syracuse University withdrew its membership from the AAU because it was reducing its emphasis on federal research dollars and was about to be voted out as well (Wilson, 2011). The flagship focus on research dollars of course discourages any emphasis on undergraduate teaching.

With competition for available research dollars going through the roof, we can expect more casualties of the research prestige wars. The banishment of Nebraska from the AAU has implications for other flagships of systems in which the medical school is located on a non-flagship campus (usually urban), particularly if the flagship does not have an engineering school. Such flagships may not generate enough federal research dollars to meet AAU standards unless they incorporate into their portfolio research dollars generated elsewhere in the system. For purposes of research funding and flagship AAU status, the system is thus "one university." For purposes of reporting retention and graduation rates, which often are not to the flagship's advantage, each campus of the system is treated separately. One example of a flagship that appears to employ this strategy is IUB. The Indianapolis campus of IU (IUPUI) generates sufficient research dollars that, when added to those generated by the Bloomington campus, is enough to maintain the latter's AAU status. An additional factor that will eventually come into play is the relative decline in research funding that will tighten the pressure on faculty and ultimately leave only a few institutions with AAU status.

Graduate Programs

Rankism can also be used to obscure or prevent the acknowledgment of research and graduate training done on campuses subordinate to flagships. A good example is the refusal of the Purdue University Graduate School to allow its programs at IUPUI to specify "Awarded for Study in Indianapolis" on the diploma of their PhD graduates, despite the fact that all of the funding and research training for these students is independently provided by IUPUI faculty. Instead, the Graduate School insists that this training be credited to the West Lafayette campus.

Community Colleges

Perhaps the most egregious rankism has been reserved for community colleges. In 2010, the *New York Times* ran a series of articles discussing why colleges are so selective. Nowhere in the discussion was there a mention of community colleges, even though there are around 1100 of them enrolling nearly half of the undergraduate population of the United States. "Dean Dad," who writes a blog for Inside Higher Ed, duly noted this omission in his post "When We Say College, We Don't Mean You" (September 13, 2010). Dean Dad is to higher education as Batman is to Gotham City. His identity was unknown until recently (see Dean Dad, 2010), but he has been a crusader for community colleges who has excellent insights into the workings of higher education. Dean Dad pointed out that the writers of the *New York Times* articles reflect a general bias that promotes class polarization because community college students are not thought of as true college students.

RESEARCH PRESTIGE AND ATHLETIC PRESTIGE: BROTHERS UNDER THE SKIN

Faculty members at Division I universities have long complained that athletic programs sully their institutions by their clearly hypocritical admission of academically unqualified students who are gifted football and basketball players. What the faculty apparently does not realize is that the quest for research prestige and the quest for athletic prestige share many of the same features and values. They are both expensive, the subject of enormous hype, driven by rankings, and the star players are treated deferentially. Scandal is common to both, but the scandals are usually less visible in research, although no less consequential.

On the research side, wannabe stars commit research misconduct such as the misappropriation of research funds and data falsification, leading to the retraction of publications and loss of federal funding. Football and basketball programs commit recruiting violations and establish slush funds for players. Criminal behavior by athletes off the field/court is common and sometimes extends to coaches, as in the Sandusky case at Penn State (for an insightful discussion of this case, see Berube, 2012).

The Division I intercollegiate athletic system is immensely powerful and many flagship university presidents have expressed despair at keeping it under institutional control. Three excellent books by Shulman and Bowen (2001), Sperber (2000), and Duderstadt (2002) have detailed the problems created by big-time intercollegiate athletics. Shulman and Bowen have provided statistics for every conceivable relationship between college sports and educational values, from admissions qualifications through program revenues and expenditures, to post-collegiate achievements of athletes. Sperber put forth the view that public flagship universities have allowed alcohol-based social events revolving around athletics ("beer and circus") to dilute serious undergraduate learning. Duderstadt has written an insightful account of how and why big-time intercollegiate athletics has become the problem it has. All of these authors are in basic agreement with one another about the kinds of difficulties posed by big-time intercollegiate athletics to universities and all have suggested solutions for these problems. Here I rely primarily on Duderstadt's keen insights as a former President of the University of Michigan, which has one of the most high profile college football programs and alumni/fan bases in the nation.

Duderstadt believes, correctly in my opinion, the basic problem with big-time intercollegiate athletics is that it feeds an insatiable public appetite for sports events, particularly football and basketball. The primary objective is winning championships, bowl games, and tournaments, immortalized in a quote by famed Green Bay Packers football coach Vince Lombardi: "Winning isn't everything, it's the only thing." Coaches that consistently win conference championships, go to bowl games or make the NCAA tournament, become icons with power that can exceed that of the university president.

Gaining control over athletics is made more difficult because big-time athletic departments operate on the fringe of the university, almost as independent entities responsible for their own financing (Duderstadt, 2002). Their financial strategy is driven by the belief that consistent winners in football and basketball make the most money and those who spend the most money win the most. The most prosperous programs set the standards for the entire intercollegiate enterprise, regardless of school size, just as research sets the academic prestige standards for all schools. Yet like research, most athletic programs require either direct or indirect subsidies from other university income streams.

Duderstadt pointed out an even greater obstacle to university control of athletics: starting three decades ago, big-time college football and basketball became virtually owned by the entertainment industry.

Coaches are now media celebrities, with salaries much higher than presidents, to which is added endorsement income and income from summer camps. Games are played almost all year round, and during basketball season, teams play twice a week for several months, with schedules crafted to accommodate television broadcast slots, thus ensuring the disruption of their academic activities. Duderstadt cites the NCAA basketball tournament (March Madness, Road to the Final Four) as the ultimate in crass commercialization, commanding attention for several weeks in March and early April. He argues that the commercialization of intercollegiate football and basketball has denied athletics its primary purpose of providing an educational experience for students beyond the classroom. He wishes to see football and basketball dissociated from the media world and reconnected to the educational mission of the university. There is nothing wrong, wrote Duderstadt (2002), with aspiring to intercollegiate athletic excellence "...as long as these aspirations are driven primarily by a concern for the opportunities offered to students rather than primarily for the reputation of the institution or for the financial bottom line." Failing to reconnect athletics to academics, he suggested one possible corrective might be to spin off the football and basketball teams from the university so that the NFL and NBA could operate them as farm teams.

According to an August 14 (2012) report issued by ESPN, the NCAA has raised the minimum high school GPA for eligibility to play Division I intercollegiate sports from 2.0 to 2.3 (a bit over a grade of "C-" on a 4.0 scale) and will also require high school athletes to complete 10 of their 16 required core courses prior to their senior year. NCAA statistics indicate that 15.3% of all university student-athletes who enrolled in 2009–2010 would not meet the new standards, but 35.2% of football players and 43.1% of basketball players would not do so. By making this change, the NCAA hopes to make a start at increasing the level of preparation of football and basketball recruits.

Raising the bar for NCAA eligibility may make little difference, however. Many elite football and basketball recruits who do not meet eligibility requirements have always been admitted to Division I schools through special routes, because these are the athletes who can help teams win and feed the fan frenzy. Furthermore, the prospects of constraining big-time intercollegiate athletics were seriously diminished in 2006 with the establishment of the game-changing Big Ten

Network (BTN) and the other conference and individual university networks that followed, insuring that the power of the athletic entertainment industry became more firmly ensconced than ever. The lucrative television deals between Big Ten conference members and the BTN provide not only enormous revenues for their athletic programs, but also serve as an outlet to advertise their research prestige, and academic and social values to prospective students, parents, and the public at large. Just say "Big Life, Big Stage, Big Ten," a catchy mantra that has been intoned by student-athletes (mainly from sports other than football or basketball!) on the BTN during commercial breaks of games, or watch "Big Ten Icons" or the "Big Ten's Greatest Games" for moments of nostalgic history and glory. Schools in Division I athletic conferences that have formed television networks are highly unlikely to give up this deep-pocket source of money and exposure. Polls of prospective students indicate that high profile athletics is a significant factor in the equation determining their choice of university to attend (Duderstadt, 2002).

Athletic success has been used to leverage academic status. Although opposed by the University of Michigan (which wanted to reign supreme in that state), President John Hanna in the late 1940s used football success to transform Michigan Agricultural College (Michigan's land grant university) into Michigan State University and fill the vacancy left in the Big Ten by the withdrawal of the University of Chicago, the only Big Ten institution to have acted on the perception that big-time athletics was detrimental to its academic mission. Success in basketball or football has raised the visibility and prestige of once-little-known institutions such as UCLA, the University of Houston, Florida State University, North Carolina State University, and Boise State University. Consider the Final Four appearances of Butler, George Mason, Louisville, Memphis State, and Houston. Smaller institutions such as these, although still a minority, can now challenge the usual national powers in basketball and even football, and beat them. Significantly, there is no "mission differentiation" imposed on intercollegiate athletics except whatever an institution chooses for itself with regard to which sports it wishes to play and at what level of competition. The same should be true on the academic side for research activity.

Athletic prestige and research prestige go hand in hand in the Big Ten athletic conference. Prior to 2011, all 11 Big Ten universities held membership in the AAU. Notre Dame had considered joining the Big Ten in 1999 to make 12 teams but declined. According to Duderstadt (2002) the declination was in part due to the fact that the members of the Big Ten felt that Notre Dame (a school that has a 96% graduation rate) did not meet the academic standards of the conference because its "...graduate and professional programs were not sufficiently distinguished to earn membership in the AAU." In 2011, the University of Nebraska, then an AAU member, became the 12th member of the Big Ten. In November of 2012, the University of Maryland and Rutgers University, both AAU members, also joined the Big Ten, extending the reach of the conference into the large East Coast market and augmenting the athletic coffers of both institutions.

As mentioned earlier, Nebraska was kicked out of the AAU in 2012 for not generating sufficient federal research dollars. This leaves one wondering whether the Big Ten should not remove Nebraska from the conference. Doing so might cause hard feelings, but not doing so might diminish the prestige of the other members! All sarcasm aside, the linkage of research prestige to athletic conference membership is simply an ultra-snobbish form of rankism we can do without. Let the geographic location and size of institutions and/or their level and quality of play determine their eligibility to join an athletic conference.

THE FUTURE OF HIGHER EDUCATION

Reading the publications and electronic newsletters that cover higher education, one senses that big changes are coming, due to the cost and ineffectiveness of the current structure and the instability being created by disruptive innovations. Although providing lifelong social and financial value, a 4-year university education is becoming progressively more expensive for middle-class families, and out of reach for poorer ones. The mad scramble of the public flagships to constantly increase their size and research prestige is not sustainable. And far too many students unfortunately choose to attend universities based on the halo effect of social, athletic, and research prestige, not knowing or caring whether or not they actually get a quality education. The future of public higher education is a choice among business as usual, tweaking around the edges, or a complete restructuring of our higher education system.

Business as Usual

We can maintain and enhance the current caste system by putting more money into the flagships to make them larger, wealthier, more exclusive, and better able to pursue research prestige. The federal government could subsidize research and graduate education in select flagships, augmented by corporate and private gifts, while states could focus their resources on undergraduate education in other public universities, augmented by student tuition and private gifts. The estimate of the flagship federal subsidy required would be between 22 and 30 billion dollars per year, in addition to the current NIH and NSF research budgets (Courant et al., 2010). M. Duane Nellis, President of the University of Idaho, points out that investment in the select few would diminish the ability of most public universities to develop their scholarly capacity (Nellis, 2009). In any event, a report from the National Academies scheduled to debut soon is expected to state that such federal largesse is unlikely (Baskin, 2012b). Instead, the report will recommend that the flagships undertake fundamental improvements, particularly in undergraduate education (see Rawlings, 2012).

I am skeptical that AAU member universities and aspirants are up to the job of making real and lasting improvements in undergraduate education, as this would mean expending less effort on research and more on teaching. Research faculty members are often unwilling to put in the time and effort required for quality undergraduate instruction, and teaching faculty are not rewarded adequately for superior performance. Although flagships report average 6-year graduation rates of around 80%, I know from experience and association that the bar is not set very high in these institutions and graduating from them is not difficult. Furthermore, a large proportion of college graduates these days appear to learn little during their undergraduate years, as documented by Arum and Roska (2011).

One flagship institution trying to become more inclusive and diverse through growth in size is Arizona State University (Blumenstyk, 2012; Hacker and Dreifus, 2010). ASU has grown to more than 70,000 students over the last decade, and its president, Michael Crow, has led an impressive effort to reorganize the university into new academic configurations that promote missions relevant to society. At the same time, however, he wants ASU to become a research powerhouse. Crow's vision reflects a common flagship institutional view that becoming mega-sized makes them better able to play a more prominent role in society. ASU is not a member of the AAU, but it aspires to invitation (see president.asu.edu/oneuniversity/what), thus committing the university to the research prestige arms race. The idea of doing it all in mega-universities where "all" tries to resolve the conflicting values of seeking research prestige vs quality education for a large and diverse student population seems pointless, as by the very nature of the academic reward system, the values of research prestige will ultimately dominate.

The National Academies' report is unlikely to deter the wealthiest flagships in their blind pursuit of research prestige, and we will see renewed efforts for privatizing. Public research universities wealthy enough through their endowments, auxiliary, and translational income, and corporate support may be able to pull it off, but privatization would raise some interesting questions. If the university is no longer supported by the state, then it is no longer a state symbol and should not be called the University of (State). A new name reflecting its private status, perhaps the name of a major philanthropic donor should be chosen. This is already the case in the Big Ten with Purdue, which is the land grant university of Indiana, but is named after John Purdue who donated the land for the university. While the football and basketball teams would not be affected *per se*, they would no longer be the "state" teams. Furthermore, in considering whether or not state-supported universities should be allowed to privatize, state legislators should factor in past investments by the state in these institutions. One can imagine schemes arising to preserve the state name on the privatized university, such as the state contributing a dollar per year in support of the university. Although clever, there would be an absurdity factor to such schemes that would need to be considered.

We can expect to see many schemes designed to perpetuate the status quo by public flagships that will cite fear of a loss of flagship research quality (especially in STEM areas) and global US research competitiveness. China is often cited as the nation likely to overtake us as they follow our lead in pouring government money into research universities. However, if China allows a higher education caste system to develop, they will inevitably face the same problems of polarization, rankism, and lack of sustainability that we do. Hopefully, they will be more far-sighted than we have been, and even more hopefully, we will recover from our myopia!

Tweak Around the Edges

One tweak that has been suggested is to establish collaborations between campuses within a system (Logue, 2010). This is an excellent idea, but is unlikely to succeed on its own because the flagship of the system must always be dominant and will disdain collaboration with the other institutions of the system, because it does not consider them a peer group. Goldrick-Rab (2012) put it well with her observation that "Instead of flagships working in tandem with sister institutions to find places for each of the state's high school graduates, they try to hog as many resources as possible, leaving other campuses to struggle with less. The greater good suffers."

A second tweak involves online learning. There is a great deal of discussion these days about the "disruptiveness" to universities of online education (Bower and Christiansen, 1995; Christiansen and Eyring, 2011), which many predict to be a game-changer in educational and financial opportunity. There are several established, for-profit online universities that award degrees based on competency examinations rather than credit hour completion. Their degrees are clearly oriented toward specific job training, as opposed to the much broader liberal education so long preferred by traditional colleges and universities. Some traditional universities such as the University of Maryland University College and the University of Massachusetts have long acted as distance education providers. We are now presented with a new idea, the MOOCs (Massively Open Online Courses). MOOCs would be designed by professors at elite universities and sold to other universities through start-up platforms such as Coursera, edX, Udemy, and Udacity (Carey, 2012; Young, 2012a,b). MOOCs have been touted as a way to increase instructional quality and decrease the costs of instruction by requiring fewer professors (Kolowich, 2012a,b; Rees, 2012).

MOOC money could theoretically free flagship research faculty even further from teaching, helping to maintain or augment research prestige. Although research universities have previously looked down on online learning, they are now embracing it and their prestige is lending it legitimacy (Young, 2012a,b). Serious attention is being paid to MOOCs by private research universities. Harvard, Princeton, Cal Tech, MIT, and Stanford have all signed on with one online platform or another to develop MOOCs, and public research universities are sure to follow. The indication is that, if a MOOC economy (or any other popular online venture) takes off and reduces costs, the elites want their brand to be at the top of the heap. In my view, however, there is no *a priori* reason to assume that MOOCs from the most prestigious research universities would be better than those emanating from un-anointed universities. Thus public universities of all kinds could be their own platform for MOOCs designed by their own professors. Ultimately, perhaps a free exchange of courses among universities might improve everyone's undergraduate curriculum.

For now, the future of MOOCS and other forms of online learning has yet to become clear. Some proponents think that the time has come for online learning to completely replace less-selective universities, leaving a two-tiered system with the elite institutions providing the traditional university education to those that can still afford it, and an online substitute for everyone else (Carlson and Blumenstyk, 2012). Others believe that the data generated by tens of thousands of online students will lead to the development of software systems that can "adapt to the needs and learning styles of individual students as they proceed through a course of instruction," thus greatly enhancing undergraduate education (Carr, 2012). My own view is that most universities will have some blended combination of face-to-face and online instruction and the institutions that best integrate these will have the most success.

Spin Off Research and Graduate Education

The seemingly incompatible missions of research and high-quality undergraduate education in flagship universities could be solved in the same way that has been proposed to deal with intercollegiate athletics. The research function could be spun off into research institutes that have no university affiliation and are financed solely by grants and private donations. Hacker and Dreifus (2010) have made a similar suggestion but would include medical schools in the separation. There are many examples of think tanks such as the Hoover Institute at Stanford and biomedical science institutes such as the Broad and Whitehead in Boston, the Stowers in Kansas City, and the cluster of Scripps, Salk, Burnham, and other institutes along Torrey Pines Road in La Jolla. All of the state universities could now focus on undergraduate education. They would all receive a certain state appropriation and charge the same tuition. Coupled with the privatizing of athletics, the formation of private research institutes would reduce university rankism because reputation would now have to be earned solely on the basis of how well the institutions performed in delivering undergraduate education.

On the other hand, an argument can be made that research and graduate education is an essential function of universities in general, but in a way that is much more synergistic and integrated with undergraduate education and service than exists in the current system. To keep research and undergraduate education together under the same roof while satisfying the need to reduce costs and the prestige arms race, however, will require a large culture change in the flagships. In a recent article on whether the current structure of higher education matches the needs of the twenty-first century, Anya Kamenetz (2010b) wrote "...there is little national will to grow our way out of this problem by founding more colleges or spending much more money on the ones we do have. Have we hit some kind of natural limit for an educated population? Or is there a mismatch between the structures of the past and the needs of the present"? My response is that there is indeed a mismatch, and that restructuring the whole system of higher education is the best way to eliminate it.

Restructure the System

The goal of restructuring would be to maximize the impact each public university can have on educational opportunity, culture, and economic development in its state, region, and the nation. To achieve this goal requires elimination of the caste system imposed by mission differentiation and its replacement with a system that allows all public institutions to *choose* the destiny they wish to chart for themselves with regard to research. If the effort to restructure our universities fails, then I would opt for separation of the research enterprise into institutes that can collaborate with universities, but are not attached to them.

In this system, undergraduate education would be the foundation mission that comes first for *all* institutions. Each public university would admit the same cross-section of students and receive the same legislative appropriations per student to partially offset tuition. The nature of a research mission would be the choice of the individual university, but this mission would not be allowed to take precedence over the educational mission. I cannot overemphasize the need for these missions to be *balanced, synergistic, and rewarded equally.* A lack of balance and inequality of rewards is one of the biggest obstacles to maximizing the effectiveness of higher education. In my view, a university that emphasizes the synergy between research and teaching gives the best service to its constituents. IUB's Tracy Sonneborn, one of America's great cell biologists of the twentieth century, was reputed to have said that first he gave the 40 h he owed to the university, after which he gave his 40 h to research. The meaning was clear: the core function of the university is undergraduate education. Research is driven by a passion connected to, but not more important than, that core function. By the simple act of holding all public universities accountable for excellence in undergraduate education, and at the same time removing political obstacles to choosing the additional mission of research and graduate education, each institution can have the maximum positive impact on the educational opportunities, culture, and economy of a state.

The massive size of many public research universities makes them inherently unwieldy and inefficient. In the restructuring process they should become smaller in order to serve these missions more effectively. It will be imperative for them to give up their insane arms race for research prestige (though not the goal of research excellence), and their rankism, and be willing to collaborate with other institutions in their states and beyond. They must give up their repression of graduate education and research in the general academic units of their regional and urban campuses, and allow them to function autonomously and, in the case of their urban campuses, in an integrated way with their professional schools. The mission of the AAU to strengthen graduate education and research must become inclusive, not exclusive, so that all may reap the benefits of this organization and should also emphasize strengthening of undergraduate education.

Lewis Pyenson (1998) has correctly observed that there is no downside to research *per se* as long as we do not neglect undergraduate education. He has advocated expanding the research doctorate to any kind of institution where the expertise and resources exist to support it, rather than restricting it to historically privileged universities. Such expansion, however, would still require academic birth control to reduce the number of PhDs on the market. A way to do this for the sciences might be to continue to award the available research dollars from federal and other agencies on the basis of merit, but to use a review mechanism that is blinded with regard to both the institution of proposal origin and the names of the proposers so that any institution or faculty member has the opportunity to compete on the merit of their ideas.

Two-year community colleges should be included in the restructuring. The academic function of community colleges is too often viewed as being primarily remedial. When Ronald A. Williams became president of Prince George's Community College, Maryland in 1999, he had a vision for Prince George's that emphasized excellence as well as access (Evelyn, 2002). For example, Williams instituted an Honors Academy for outstanding students, who can hold dual admission with any of four institutions in Maryland and Washington, DC. The current president of St. George's, Charlene M. Dukes, has continued this emphasis on academic excellence, as have other community college leaders, a trend that should continue. There is also no reason why community college faculty and students should not conduct research if they so choose and have the infrastructure to support it.

This new structure would have a number of benefits for public higher education (Stocum, 2000, 2001). First, it would harness the full educational power and expertise of the state universities in training a multileveled work force to meet the state's economic needs. Second, it would send the message to all students—whether they are engaged in technical training or pursuing a course of doctoral study—that their education is seen as valuable by the state as a whole. Third, it would make course credit transfer between institutions easier, which in some states is a problem because the flagships resist accepting credits from "inferior" institutions, even ones within their own systems. Fourth, more expertise would be brought to bear on the problem of student retention and graduation rates, because this problem would now belong to everyone and everyone would have a stake in it. It would eliminate the corrosive effects stemming from the abuse of institutions lower in the caste order by higher education commissions, state legislatures, and university trustees. Fifth, the full economic and cultural power of the deep pool of faculty research talent and expertise could be applied over a much broader area of the state. Furthermore, the diversity of research ideas generated by faculty would be increased, generating more technology transfer and providing a greater cultural resource. Sixth, with such a structure, states would have multiple connection points for national and world educational commerce, rather than one or two. Seventh, this structure would make it much easier to join with the K-12 system in setting standards of student preparation for university work and teacher training, and in forming collaborations to address educational issues.

In short, this structure would recommit to doing what the original land grant universities were designed to do, but with a more global range of responsibilities and using modern technological tools. The universities would not be operating in isolation from one another, but rather in networks enabled by the greater collaboration between institutions made possible by the increased flexibility of this structure, thus maximizing the investments made in the higher education system.

There would undoubtedly be fierce resistance to such changes from the faculty, administrators, and trustees of flagship universities accustomed to relative privilege, from their alumni and students whose identities are wrapped up in their school's symbols and prestige rankings, and from the politicians who perpetuate the status quo. To achieve the goal, a new generation of bold leaders will be needed to populate legislatures, higher education governing bodies, university boards, and university administrations. These leaders must place high value on personal and institutional integrity, possess a decent humility, and above all be courageous in the face of countervailing forces if they are to make an authentic impact.

DEFINING THE PURPOSE OF UNDERGRADUATE EDUCATION

If excellence in undergraduate education is to be the core of a restructured higher education system, we must develop a clear idea of the purpose of higher education, which today appears to be progressively more consumerist and vocational. Charles Grosvenor Osgood (1871–1964), Holmes Professor of Belles Lettres at Princeton University, put this purpose succinctly: "The supreme end of education is expert discernment in all things—the power to tell the good from the bad, the genuine from the counterfeit, and to prefer the good and the genuine to the bad and the counterfeit." We pursue this end through learning—by study, through experience, by discovery, and, most importantly of all, from mistakes and failures. Learning is the most important process we engage in throughout our lives, and brings wisdom. The nature of the curriculum that defines what is to be learned is the subject of other discourse; here, I wish only to comment on learning as the fundamental purpose of undergraduate education.

Nowhere have I seen a better statement on the value of learning than in Josef Martin's (1988) book *To Rise Above Principle: Memoirs of an Unreconstructed Dean*. Martin writes: "Biologically, humans are not all that special...it is culturally that human beings are very special indeed. So to become human means to become cultured: it means to learn about humanity's history and its science, literature, and arts; it means to become aware of what the best minds have thought about human existence."

Martin asks, what do we in the academic community stand for? He answers, "We stand for learning...for its own sake...and we insist that nothing else is so relevant. 'Relevant to what' we may be asked? Relevant to all aspects of human life is the answer we should give. Learning...instills some important values. It instills honesty, because there is no such thing as dishonest learning...learning is a hard taskmaster; in fact, there is no way to beat the system: you learn honestly or you don't learn at all.

Learning offers ample opportunity to acquire a decent humility. Those who attempt to learn honestly can hardly fail to acknowledge their own limitations...further, one can hardly love and practice learning without acquiring some respect for the differing opinions of others, because honest learning so often demonstrates that we change from our earlier views.

But chiefly the commitment to learning for its own sake, to scholarship, and the search for truth is itself a very strong statement of values held and advocated. It is, moreover, a statement of values consistent with the values of this republic and its constitution. It advocates education rather than indoctrination; it manifests the faith that free and well-educated people will not succumb to authoritarian or totalitarian dogma."

Then Martin makes what I think is his most important statement: "...the best preparation we can give our children is to teach them as much as possible of what we have learned about humanity and about nature and to make them aware of the seduction of dogma, of the wishfulness that can cause us to accept some beliefs against our better judgment. We must bring ourselves and our children as far as possible to think analytically and critically."

THE URBAN UNIVERSITY AS A MODEL FOR THE TWENTY-FIRST CENTURY

Is there a model we might use as a starting point to reclaim the original land grant vision of Justin Morrill? In his book *An Education for Our Time* (1998), Josiah Bunting III, President Emeritus of the Virginia Military Institute and President of the H. Frank Guggenheim Foundation, argues for the establishment of a fictive new kind of university, located on the high plains of Wyoming and focused on the development of student character and morality rather than vocational and technical aims. I believe we could combine these features in the model represented by today's urban public university, which Donald Langenberg, former Chancellor of the University of Maryland, said in his keynote speech celebrating the 20th anniversary of the founding of IUPUI is "...bringing to the cities the populist land grant spirit that propelled our older state universities to greatness. It is upon these urban universities that the future of our cities, and hence our nation, depends."

This may sound surprising, as most urban public universities are little known, underfunded, and viewed as serving primarily students who need little intellectual stimulation. Nevertheless, it is they who best fit the balance of activities that address the needs and challenges society will face in the twenty-first century. Urban universities have a high level of student diversity and are deeply committed to undergraduate learning. They do both basic and applied research that is often of direct and immediate relevance to broad societal issues, such as addiction, health care, and poverty. Urban universities have a deep sense of both internal and external communities. For these reasons, a number of such universities across the country are emerging as leaders in integrating teaching, research, and service into a balanced whole that serves their state, national, and global constituents with the maximum impact. It is no coincidence that most of these are not part of a flagship-led system, but are independent and in charge of their own destiny.

A prime example is the University of Maryland Baltimore County (UMBC), led by its president, Freeman Hrabowski III (Hacker and Dreifus, 2010). UMBC has a highly diverse student body that is known for producing graduates in the sciences and engineering, but also in the liberal arts. It has been described as one of the best up and coming universities in the country for several years running because it personifies what research coupled with excellence in teaching can do for its students. UMBC and its counterparts, then, is an emerging evolutionary prototype by which higher education in the twenty-first century can be transformed to truly provide our citizens with "an education for our time," while responding to the research needs of the nation.

REFERENCES

Alberts, B., 2010. Overbuilding research capacity. Science 329, 1257.

Alpert, D., 1993. Rethinking the challenges facing the American research university.
This unpublished manuscript is an excellent discussion of the dissonances facing research universities in the 1990s. The manuscript is part of the Daniel Alpert papers, 1941–1998, in the University of Illinois Archives. Alpert is Emeritus Professor of Physics, Emeritus Dean of the Graduate College, and Emeritus Director of the Center for Advanced Study, University of Illinois Urbana-Champaign.

National Association of American Universities. Wikipedia, accessible at http://en.wikipedia.org/wiki/Association_of_American_Universities

Anderson, M., 1992. Imposters in the Temple. Simon and Schuster, New York.

Arum, R., Roska, J., 2011. Academically Adrift. University of Chicago Press, Chicago, IL.

Astin, A., 1999. Rethinking academic excellence. Liberal Education. Spring Issue, pp. 10–18.

Baskin, P., 2011. Ranking of research universities may harm more than Nebraska. The Chronicle of Higher Education, May 13.

Baskin, P., 2012a. Public no longer? NSF sounds alarm over cuts at state research universities. The Chronicle of Higher Education, October 5.

Baskin, P., 2012b. Panel on research universities sees need for fundamental changes. The Chronicle of Higher Education, March 9.

Bergom I, Waltman J (2009) Satisfaction and discontent: voices of non-tenure-track faculty. Association of American Colleges and Universities, Vol 37, Number 3 (Winter issue, On Campus with Women).

Berrett, D., 2011. What's next for Wisconsin? Inside Higher Ed, June 6.

Berube, M., 2012. Why I resigned the Paterno Chair. The Chronicle of Higher Education, Review, October 19.

Blumenstyk, G., 2012. Change takes root in the desert. The Chronicle of Higher Education, November 23.

Bower, J.L., Christensen, C.M., 1995. Disruptive technologies: catching the wave. Harv. Bus. Rev. January–February.

Boyte, H., Hollander, E., 1999. Wingspread declaration on renewing the civic mission of the American Research University. Johnson Foundation, Racine, WI.

Bunting III, J., 1998. An Education for Our Time. Regnery Publishing, Washington, DC.

Carey, K., 2011. Why flagship public universities should stay public. The Chronicle of Higher Education, August 12.

Carey, K., 2012. Revenge of the underpaid professors. The Chronicle of Higher Education, May 25.

Carneval, A.P., Strohl, J., 2011. Our economically polarized college system: separate and unequal. The Chronicle of Higher Education, September 10.

Carlson, S., Blumenstyk, G., 2012. The false promise of the education revolution. The Chronicle of Higher Education, December 21.

Carr, N., 2012. The crisis in higher education. MIT Technol. Rev. 115 (8), 32–40.

Christensen, C.M., Eyring, H.J., 2011. The Innovative University. Jossey-Bass, San Francisco, CA.

Committee on Institutional Cooperation (1989) Values Added: Undergraduate Education at the Universities of the CIC. Office of Public Affairs/Office of Publications of the University of Illinois at Urbana-Champaign.

Courant, P.N., Duderstadt, J.J., Goldenberg, E.N., 2010. Needed: a national strategy to preserve public research universities. The Chronicle of Higher Education, January 8.

Culpepper, T.A., 2006. The myth of inferiority. The Chronicle of Higher Education Review, October 27.

Cyranoski, D., Gilbert, N., Ledford, H., Nayer, A., Yahia, M., 2011. The PhD factory. Nature 472, 276–279.

Dean Dad, 2010. When we say "college", we don't mean you. Inside Higher Ed, September 13. Dean Dad revealed his secret identity in his blog post of November 13, 2012. He is Matt Reed, VP for Academic Affairs at Holyoke Community College in Holyoke, MA. Prior to 2007, he was Dean of Liberal Arts at the County College of Morris in Randolph, NJ.

Duderstadt, J.J., 2002. Intercollegiate Athletics and the American University. The University of Michigan Press, Ann Arbor, MI.

Evelyn, J., 2002. An elite vision. The Chronicle of Higher Education, October 4.

Fuller, R.W., 2004. Somebodies and Nobodies. Rankism and the Abuse of Rank. New Society Publishers, BC, Canada.

Goldrick-Rab, S., 2012. Strengthening systems would improve public higher education (essay). Inside Higher Ed, October 4.

Gose, B., 2002. The fall of the flagships. The Chronicle of Higher Education, July 5.

Hacker, A., Dreifus, C., 2010. Higher Education? How Colleges Are Wasting Our Money and Failing Our Kids—and What We Can Do About it. Times Books, New York, NY.

Hattie, J., Marsh, H.W., 1996. The relationship between research and teaching: a meta-analysis. Rev. Educ. Res. 66, 507–542.

Hattie J and Marsh H (2004) One journey to unravel the relationship between research and teaching. Research and Teaching: Closing the Divide? An International Colloquium, Winchester, Hampshire, March 18–19. Accessible at http://www.education.auckland.ac.nz.

Haycock, K., Lynch, M., Engle, J., 2010. Opportunity adrift. The Education Trust, January.

Julius, D.J., 2011. When systems evolve. Inside Higher Ed, June 3.

Kahlenberg, R.D., 2012. Has higher education become an engine of inequality? The Chronicle of Higher Education Review, June 6.

Kamenetz, A., 2010a. DIYU. Chelsea Green Publishing, White River Jct, VT.

Kamenetz, A., 2010b. Adapt or decline. Inside Higher Ed, March 26.

Katz, S.N., 2002. The path-breaking, fractionalized, uncertain world of knowledge. The Chronicle of Higher Education Review, September 20.

Kolowich, S., 2012a. Into the fray. Inside Higher Ed, July 17.

Kolowich, S., 2012b. "Conventional" online universities consider strategic response to MOOCs, Inside Higher Ed, August 2.

Leshner, A.I., Fluharty, S.J., 2012. Time and money are being wasted in the lab. The Chronicle of Higher Education, December 7.

Logue, A.W., 2010. The power of the system. Inside Higher Ed, May 21.

MacDougall, M., 2012. Research-teaching linkages: beyond the divide in undergraduate medicine. Int. J. Sch. Teach. Learn. 6, 1–21.

Martin J., 1988. To Rise Above Principle. University of Illinois Press, Urbana and Chicago.
Josef Martin is the pen name of Henry H. Bauer, a respected chemist who served as Dean of Arts and Sciences, and Professor of Sciences and Chemistry at Virginia Tech University until his retirement in 1999.

Martinson, B.C., 2007. Universities and the money fix. Nature 449, 141–142.

Nellis, M.D., 2009. The wrong rescue plan. Inside Higher Ed, December 15.

Nelson, L.A., 2011. Examining the AAU gatekeepers. Inside Higher Ed, May 11.

Nichol, G.R., 2008. Public universities at risk: abandoning their mission. The Chronicle of Higher Education, October 31.

Parker, L.L., Greenbaum, D.A., Pister, K.S., 2001. Rethinking the land-grant research university for the digital age. Change January/February, p.12.

Pyenson, L., 1998. The liberation of higher learning. CGS Commun. XXXI (4), April.

Quiggen, J., 2011. Cutthroat admissions and rising inequality: a vicious duo. The Chronicle of Higher Education Review, September 16.

Rawlings, H.R., 2012. Essay: research universities must pay more attention to student learning. Inside Higher Ed, March 30.

Rees, J., 2012. Essay on whether online education will make professors obsolete. Inside Higher Ed, July 30.

Reich, R.B., 2000. How selective colleges heighten inequality. The Chronicle of Higher Education Review, September 15.

Remler D.K., Pema E., 2009. Why do institutions of higher education reward research while selling education? Working paper 14974 of the National Bureau of Economic Research. <http://www.nber.org/papers/w14974>.

Rhode, D.L., 2006. In Pursuit of Knowledge: Scholars, Status and Academic Culture. Stanford University Press, Palo Alto, CA.

Rhodes, F.H.T., 2006. Give us the tools. The Chronicle of Higher Education, September 1.

Schrecker, E., 2010. The Lost Soul of Higher Education: Corporatization, the Assault on Academic Freedom and the American University. The New Press, New York, NY.

Shulman, J.L., Bowen, W.G., 2001. The Game of Life. Princeton University Press, Princeton, NJ, 447 pp.

Skinner, R.A., Miller, M.R., 2012. The new research university chief(s). Inside Higher Ed, January 20.

Smith, P., 1990. Killing the Spirit. Penguin Books, New York, NY, 315 pp.

Sperber, M., 2000. Beer and Circus. Henry Holt & Co, New York, NY, 322 pp.

Stocum D.L., 2000. Urban universities: a model for the twentyfirst century. Vital Speeches of the Day LXVI, #23, 715–718.

Stocum, D.L., 2001. The evolution of twenty first century higher education: the urban university as prototype. Metrop. Univ. J. 12, 10–19.

Tuchman, G., 2009. Wannabe U.. University of Chicago Press, Chicago, IL,.
Wannabe U is widely thought to be the University of Connecticut.

Undergraduate Research as a Deep Learning Experience, College of Arts and Sciences Undergraduate Research Advisory Committee, 2006. Available from http://www2.winthrop.edu/artscience/undergradresearch/new_page_2.htm

Wilson, R., 2010. Why teaching is not priority number1. The Chronicle of Higher Education, September 10.

Wilson, R., 2011. Syracuse's slide. The Chronicle of Higher Education, Oct 7.

Young, J.R., 2012a. Inside the Coursera contract. The Chronicle of Higher Education, August 3.

Young, J.R., 2012b. MOOCs take a major step toward qualifying for college credit. The Chronicle of Higher Education November 23, A23.

www.ingramcontent.com/pod-product-compliance
Lightning Source LLC
Chambersburg PA
CBHW071416290426
44108CB00014B/1855